Katie Hanlon has lived on the South Coast of Devon all her life, and discovered her passion for writing at nine years old. She became a carer for her mother at age thirteen, which became one of the main reasons for Katie to start writing poetry. Now at age twenty-two, she has released her first poetry book to share her experiences.

This book of poetry is dedicated to Mum, Dad, and Cheryl, who have always supported me.

Katie Hanlon

JUDGE MY SOUL

AUSTIN MACAULEY PUBLISHERS®
LONDON · CAMBRIDGE · NEW YORK · SHARJAH

Copyright © Katie Hanlon 2025

The right of Katie Hanlon to be identified as author of this work has been asserted by the author in accordance with sections 77 and 78 of the Copyright, Designs and Patents Act 1988.

All rights reserved. No part of this publication may be reproduced, stored in a retrieval system, or transmitted in any form or by any means, electronic, mechanical, photocopying, recording, or otherwise, without the prior permission of the publishers.

Any person who commits any unauthorised act in relation to this publication may be liable to criminal prosecution and civil claims for damages.

A CIP catalogue record for this title is available from the British Library.

ISBN 9781035884216 (Paperback)
ISBN 9781035884223 (ePub e-book)

www.austinmacauley.com

First Published 2025
Austin Macauley Publishers Ltd®
1 Canada Square
Canary Wharf
London
E14 5AA

A Day in My Life

Cry myself to sleep,
Cry myself awake,
No one hears my pain.

Check my phone every morning,
No new messages,
No one cares about my situation.

Work all day,
Hide behind a smile,
No one asks how my day was.

Speak to the therapist,
That's 50 pounds an hour,
No one wants to listen.

Heart feels empty,
Head feels cold,
Happiness is fleeting,
No one cares how I am feeling.

Arguments

It bottles and builds,
Boils and bubbles,
Like lava and magma,
It explodes and flows,
Or fizzes and pounds,
Like soda in an unopened can,
Shake it and bang!
It overflows and tingles,
Like a waterfall,
The water gathers to the edge,
Over it goes.

It swirls into a storm,
Of insults and terrible words,
Of back and forth,
Of swearing unlike any other,
It manifests into a demon,
Red face, eyes ablaze, harsh voices.
Two faces close together,
Hands clenched and ready to throw.

And all of a sudden,
It stops,
Abrupt and left on the wrong words,
Heartbroken and in tears,
The bed cold and empty,
Backs face each other,
The distance widens,
Hearts and minds heal and wounds close.
"I'm sorry, so sorry, I didn't mean what I said last night. Forgive me?"

"Hardly," she said.

Betrayal

Take a knife, a dagger, a sword
Made of words.
Engage in psychological warfare,
Recruit your army
Made up of desperate worship and sacrifice,

Win the court's favour,
For when the time comes, slip the poison into the wine,
To watch as I choke on sadness and disappointment,
To bury my memory into your subconscious,

For when you take the crown and sit upon the throne of blood,
As the army caters to your every whim.
Will you look at my poisoned heart, my broken body, my self-sabotaging brain,
With despair and regret,
Or will it remind you of your victory?

All this time, old friend, I trusted you with everything.

Freedom

You can have my body,
You can have my blood,
You can have my brain,
But you will never have my heart.

Study each scar thoroughly,
For the flame behind my eyes is lost,
The pain you have caused,
It's eternal.

When I am dead,
This cold cage will disintegrate,
And I will fly free,
Guided by the warmth of the sun.

I Am Fire

From the ashes,
Rose an ember,
It glowed a brilliant orange,
And set the skies ablaze.

From a spark,
Stood a flame,
It cracked like a whip,
And bolted through the air.

From the dense smoke,
Signalled an inferno,
It spread like an infection,
And turned the land into hell.

I am fire,
Do not underestimate me

I Need You

You are my shield against the onslaught of
Life.
You are the needle that stitched my heart
Together.
You are the shoulder that my tears dried
On.

You are the oxygen that my lungs
Need.
You are the joy that ignites my
Brain.
You are the lifeline on the heart
Monitor.

You are the sun that hangs in the
Sky.
You are the pulse that runs in my
Veins.
I need you but do you need
Me?

Is It Too Hard to Have Faith in Me?

I can see it in your eyes,
The black iris of disappointment,
Surrounded by green scepticism,
The tone shifted,

Every time I speak,
The stonewalls rise up higher,
My opinion falls by the wayside,
Your opinion is a parasite

That infects my brain,
My emotions dull,
The stars in my eyes fade,
Why don't you tell me what to do?

Even if you did,
I would still be wrong,
My compass switches directions
Because of your parasite.

My heart fails
Because of your poison,
I hate myself
Because without you,
I'm nothing.

Judge My Soul

A soul enters the Duat.
"Anubis, take my heart."
With ease, he places the heart on the scale,
My heart falls to the floor,
Failing the test against Ma'at,
Ammit opens her mouth
Revealing the rows of sharp crooked teeth.
Anubis takes my heart,
And feed it to his demon.
Dying a second time doesn't feel so bad.

A new soul enters the Duat.
"Anubis, take my heart."
He places the heart on the scale,
The feather falls to the floor,
Horus gestures to me,
I follow,
And he guides me to Osiris.
The god of the Duat.
Sitting upon a throne he casts judgment.
Aaru is open to me.

Osiris speaks with such command,
"The journey is long and perilous.
You are not the only one on this voyage.
Many demons and deities guard a never-ending amount of gates."

I just need to get through
Then the boat will be rowed across the water
To the shores of the Field of Reeds.
Boundless reed fields across a series of islands.
Where the perfect paradise awaits us.

Just a Movie Scene

It was just like a movie scene,
The heavens opened,
Hitting the glass of the bus stop,
Flooding the street with pools of sorrow.

Her eyes kept catching mine,
I couldn't deny the attraction,
Brown eyes and soaked dark hair,
She had no coat, nothing to protect her

From the tears of angels.
Every time we crossed, I could hear her voice
Begging for shelter to cover her shivering body.
I caved, offering her my coat,

As I now stood in my shirt,
I will never forget her smile and her thankful eyes.
As the bus came into view,
It warmed me,

We spent a few months getting close,
With a relationship put on the table,
And one consenting party,
It seemed like fate.

But wait, a catch, a boy she was caught with.
She had two offers.
It's just like a movie,
A typical romance,

A girl who has to choose between two lovers,
But the ending was nothing like I imagined.

She chose him.
I chose to forget,
I chose not to shed any tears,
Months passed.

I never saw her face again,
Maybe it was just a movie scene.

La La Loser

"La La Loser."
Is what the children sing
Pointing and laughing at
The weird ones.

"She has no friends, how sad!"
The mean girls cackle
When they walk past
The loner.

"What's wrong with him?"
The boys snicker in the
Locker room closing in on
The nerd.

The weird ones, the loner, and the nerd all
Go to the highest authority they know.
"Ignore them, they will stop eventually."
What great advice we have received.

The children, the mean girls, and the boys
All walk past the same old posters
That means nothing.
Ripping them off the walls, an idea sparks.

The poster is shoved into our faces,
"We heard you told on us.
Guess we will have to stop bullying you,"
They say with a sadistic grin.

They call us names, lock us into lockers,
Ostracise us from any future friends,
Destroy our self-esteem,
Leave us behind in a haze of paranoia.

And they just get to walk away.

Let's Meet for a Coffee

I'll see you there,
At our usual meeting place,
Usual time,
Don't be late, smiley face (I don't send kisses).

At the door, look inside to find you,
Nervous despite the fact that I have met you there before,
Hesitate to open the door,
Reluctantly, I enter and slowly find a table.

The sounds of chatter and cups,
Shoot straight through into my brain, (it's painful), it's too bright,
Stuttering when I order a hot chocolate,
Finally, I found a table.

You walk in, radiating confidence,
Grinning with happiness (I hope),
Sit down and take off your coat,
Drape it over the chair with grace.

You lead the conversation,
I listen and add my piece if needed,
It's hot, I should have taken off my coat,
Meekly, I take it off and drape it over the chair.

The cups and plates chat amongst themselves,
Everyone is shouting,
Echoing off the walls,
I wince slightly at each sound.

"Do you want to leave?" she asks.
"Yes, please."
She smiles and takes my hand,
Lead me to the door.

A breath of fresh air,
Sense cleared,
The sun blinds me
But it looks so beautiful on you.

"Let's meet for coffee again next week?"
"You mean hot chocolate, right?" She winks.
I smile. "Yes, let's meet again.
For hot chocolate."

Lonely Is What I Am

The need to survive drives the empty husk
Through the cold winter night.

The sky settled and darkened
With every passing minute.

This husk had just left
One of their favourite places.

But the usual joy, it gave
Was slowly drained away.

Every step home felt heavy and disinterested.
The heart felt numb.

Every breath filled the husk with ice.
The mind is filled with familiar thoughts.

Desire for love, companionship,
Someone to trust and confide in.

Like an infection,
This thought spread and slowed the husk.

The basic need for survival, for food,
Water, and shelter, were enough to drive the husk home.

Once home, the husk imagined
What their potential partner would be like.

The husk contemplated their voice,
Eyes, personality, and warmth.

Before crushing defeat echoed
Through their heart and soul.

The sea of sadness drifted from their eyes,
Onto their clothes.

Looking around the home
Something was made abundantly clear.

The husk is truly alone.

Oh Blossom Tree

Oh blossom tree, how beautiful you are.
We wait all year just to see your flowers.
And just when we forget, spring rolls around.
Our patience is rewarded with your entrance.

When the time comes, those bulbs open.
Your days of bloom may only be temporary.
But the image, God, is everlasting.
Those fragile flowers cling through the breeze.

But soon, the flowers lose their grip.
And once they let go their journey begins.
The petals fall, just like snow.
Covering the ground in pink and white.

Through the warm days, and cold nights.
The trees keep flowering.
But the petals, they still fall.
Sprinkling the streets and the cars.

The petals bring us joy, only for a moment.
A brief relief from the stress of life.
For hope lies in those petals, ever fleeting as the colours fade.
But remember that they will be back.

Marriage

'Til death do us part,
That is what you said to me.
Engrave it onto my heart,
And now look at what you see.

My youth is fading away,
Broken dreams, forgotten.
The rising sun signalling a new day,
Our love lay rotten.

Sometimes I wonder,
The value of this ring.
And I ponder,
The old joy you used to bring.

But I realised early on,
The seeds of our young.
Carry onwards and mourn,
Until their songs are sung.

Mr Moon

Are you lonely up there?
Your celestial eyes peering down,
Whilst ours look up.
Your brilliance pierces through the black sky.

Are you guiding us?
Commanding the sky to light up,
A sea of glistening symbols,
Your presence is always known.

Are you in control?
The waves bow to your presence,
Crashing and breaking at your every desire,
Your name, clouded in mystery.

Are you going to harm us?
So many stories connected to you,
Supernatural beings with power that many of us desire,
Your thoughts, desires, and abilities, unknown.

Are you like me?
Misunderstood.
Illusioned.
Misfit.
Angry.
Damned.
Of course not,

You're just a grey rock,
Floating millions of miles away,
Isolated in the infinite void,
Oh, Mr Moon, we are so wrong about you.

Myself

My body is a battery,
But it is never full.

My brain is a machine,
But it is never turned off.

My heart is a target,
But no one will ever shoot for it.

My will is a butterfly,
But it is fleeting and fragile.

My love is plenty,
But it is always taken advantage of.

My blood is a battlefield,
But the casualties are chemical.

I, myself, yearn for something more,
But immortality is chosen by people.

Pristine Perfect House

Sitting in the nicest part of town
Is the pristine perfect house
With it's painted walls
And a particular garden.

No plant too tall
Or too short,
Only perfect plants are allowed
In this garden.

Ones with pretty feminine features
And plants that protect and serve,
They must have a purpose so they can
Fit in perfectly.

The gardener is very particular
And protective over his garden,
"There is no room for that plant,"
He points to one.

This flower, although feminine, is not enough,
With its wild mixture of pink and blue,
With its peculiar interest,
This flower is not perfect enough.

Reflection

Have you ever stared into a puddle?
The reflection ripples and distorts.
I can't help but wonder what the puddle thinks.

Does it stare back at me?
Through a shattered dimension.
Thinking and examining.

What is on the other side?
Just crushed stone and gravel.
Or an escape.

Why do you mock me?
Behind this pristine portal,
Lies a broken glass.

Stare into my soul and cast judgment,
For I know it's worth nothing.

Safe place

My bedroom holds my heart,
Here no one judges or
Misreads my intentions.

The walls can be covered with whatever,
Colour or a poster
It all has a place here.

My old teddy bears on my wardrobe,
Can hear my secrets
And they will never tell.

The door marks my safe place,
Open or shut
My privacy is safe (kind of).

My bedroom is my happy place,
If I could spend the rest of my life here
Then I would.

Here I could disappear
From the outside world
And stay in my safe place.

Snake

One night, it appeared,
Small, weak, and manageable,
I didn't notice it.

Slowly, over the years,
It grew, slithering along,
Constricting, twisting, and squeezing.

Now I feel it,
Around my neck, it chokes me,
I'm barely breathing.

Only hanging on because of responsibility,
It never bites,
Even if the snake wants to.

It just, ever so slowly,
Wraps around my life,
And strangles me.

Social Anxiety

My bedroom is a prison,
But it keeps me safe,
Safe from the judgment
And awkwardness,

Anxiety has chained me to the bed,
Suicidal thoughts nailed to my head,
Curtains are drawn to reduce the light
So just let me sleep off the pain.

The vibrations of music drown out my thoughts,
Restore my sanity
For I am suffering
From social anxiety.

Another missed social gathering,
But I can't get out of bed,
Can someone save me
From this torture?

I should just curl up and die.

Can't go to work
Without feeling my heart
Burst out of my chest.
Why am I like this?
Suffering alone in my prison again.

Counting the days to my next
Appointment with my therapist
So I can bleed out.

Losing focus,
Stressed out of my mind,
With no one to talk to,
I'm going to die alone.

Crying only four or five times a year,
This isn't healthy,
So I sacrifice my thoughts to
These pages.

Please someone,
Anyone,
Save me,
From myself.

Tattoo

Engrave my skin
With all the patterns I desire.
Expose my sin
So I can wear my attire.

Made of ink
And illustrated with colour.
To the brink
It begins to rupture.

Bring to life
With shadow and shade.
Full of strife
It will never fade.

On my body
For all that have admired.
Filled with envy
For the new confidence I have acquired.

The Child's Drawing

Held up by a magnet.
(The one they get from a holiday),
Is my drawing.

The background, blue and green,
With a big shining sun,
And a fluffy white cloud.

A poorly drawn house, slightly slanted,
Sat in the middle,
With a green garden.

In the garden, is the family,
Mommy, daddy, brother, dog, and me.
The dog, a brown and white smudge.

My mommy is blonde with a blue dress,
My daddy is brunette with a black shirt,
My brother is a reflection of Daddy.

They all stand, holding hands,
With the dog that sitting next to Mommy,
But I stand next to them.

I do not hold their hands,
I do not play with them,
I do not fit.

Please look at my drawing,
And understand its meaning.
For my drawing speaks a thousand words.

The Crossroads of Fate

Do you believe in fate?
That some all-knowing and all-seeing force
Has planned every second of your life.
Or perhaps they simply give you a choice.

This force places you at the crosswords.
Waiting patiently, with bated breath,
It watches you fumble, succeed, and fail,
It knows you so well by now,

That it can predict your every move.
Uncertainty and fear is your enemy,
But a friend of fate.
It clouds every road and obscures your judgment.

Why blame fate?
We are always the root of our downfall.
At the crossroads of fate,
It is always our decision that has the greatest impact.

There Is a Demon in My Heart

Make it dance,
Squeeze it, constrict it, and twist it,
Pull the lever and let's go into overdrive.

Make it hard to breathe,
Squash it, shorten it, and sabotage it,
Push the button and tighten my chest.

Make it overheat,
Ignite it, fuel it, and break it,
Turn the dial and put it into the red.

Make it churn,
Turn it, flip it, and overfill it,
Input the code and it will retch out.

Make it hard to sleep,
Exhaust it, drown it, and kill it,
Stand back and watch the meltdown.

Seven Deadly Sins

The mirror could not cast your gaze away from yourself,
A bloated body overfilled with self-love,
Ego higher than the clouds,
But you have no ability to climb them.

Hoard your treasure in the back of the cave,
Filled with cheap plastic,
And rotting sentiments,
It's all wasting away.

Seething under the surface,
Behind red-tinted sunglasses,
Is the fire that has filled your soul,
Threatening to unleash and vanquish all who oppose you.

Your gaze is tinted green,
You want, you wish, and you desire,
For what others have is something you can never gain,
They are just so much better, you tell yourself.

Love hearts in your eyes,
A window into your world,
You want that boy, that one too, and that one too,
"And nothing will stop you," you say with a creepy smile.

Slumped into a chair,
Static playing on repeat in your brain,
So drown your sorrows and trauma,
With more alcohol and food.

A mountain of hardship stands before you,
You know you chip away at it,
And become something greater,
But instead, you slip into the shadows of laziness.

Fake Friends

All my friends are fake,
From their plastic faces
And their painted smiles.

Only see them in class,
Never on the weekends
And they avoid me in the halls.

They watch when I bleed,
Pretending to care
But disappear when I need them.

I buy them lunch when they need it,
But when I forget mine
They just ignore me.

My heart is all in,
But theirs were never
There to begin with.

It is my fault,
I trust too much
And don't know when to quit

Until it's too late.
Until they show their colours,
Until they voice their true intentions.

I tell myself to hold back,
To not reveal my deck
Until the right moment.

I always seem to fall for fake friends,
Guess I overlook the warnings
To notice their war-torn red flags.

Venn Diagram

We are so different,
Like two sides of the same coin
Like the sun and the moon
Like the ocean and the sky.

One side represents power,
One side represents weakness,
But common ground can be found
In the middle.

Power and weakness
Can combine to
Create strength.

We are so different,
And so similar.

Scanning Fruit

The school counsellor has that look,
You know the one,
The look of a cashier scanning fruit,

Listening to a hundred other kids before you,
Hearing the same story,
Just like that cashier

Saying, "Do you have a rewards card?"
A thousand times,
Never caring about the response.

The school counsellor prepares their speech,
Just ticking boxes I suppose.
"So, how are you feeling today?"

I feel like in a school with hundreds of other kids,
That I am just another fruit to label.
Chucked into another box,

Labelled, so I can be packaged and sold
Under damaged goods.
What do you say to that?

Birthday

The colour of excitement
Is a red circle on a calendar,
Marking the event of such
Importance,

Even when we are one year older,
Excitement runs red in our veins,
Just like a balloon
It could burst at any moment,

Unlike a candle,
When extinguished grey excitement
Still rises,
Just waiting to share,

Whether it's a large decorated cake,
Or a rainbow of wrapping paper
At our feet,
Excitement marks a very special day indeed.